WORKBOOK

WHO GOT The KEYS?

BUILDING GENERATIONAL WEALTH Through REAL ESTATE

Donna J. Rogers

Published by R Legacy Publishing

Cover design by University of Moguls Publishing and Design
www.universityofmoguls.com

ISBN-13: 978-0-578-66312-8

For speaking engagements and bulk book orders:
Donna J. Rogers
drogers@rlegacyrealty.com

www.whogotthekeys.com
www.rlegacyrealty.com

Instagram: @realtordonnajr
Facebook: facebook.com/realtordonnajr

Dedication

This book is dedicated to my parents, John and Donna Sr. Rogers, who passed me the keys to unlock my purpose—to empower others through education and real estate.

I love and appreciate you dearly.

Table of Contents

This workbook is best used with the book:

Who Got the Keys?

Building Generational Wealth through Real Estate

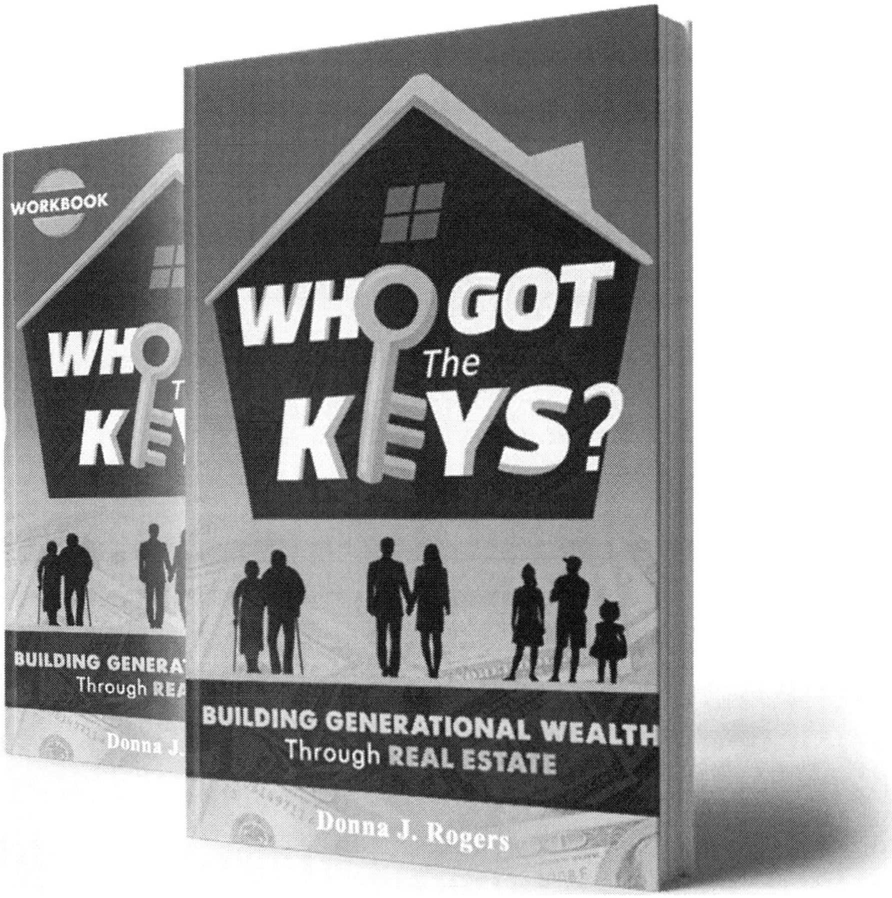

www.whogotthekeys.com

CHAPTER ONE

KEEPING IT REAL ABOUT REAL ESTATE

The Basics of Real Estate and Building Wealth

KEEPING IT REAL ABOUT REAL ESTATE AND WEALTH BUILDING

QUESTIONS FOR DISCUSSION

KEY: Understand the basics of real estate and wealth building
Answer the questions below.

1. What is the purpose of a key?

   ____

2. What is real estate?

   ____

3. Who can own real estate?

   ____

4. Name one benefit of owning real estate.

   ____

5. What is an asset?

   ____

6. What is Webster's definition of "wealth"?

   ____

7. What is author Donna's definition of "wealth"?

   ____

8. Why is it important to invest in real estate at a young age?

   ____

REAL ESTATE TYPES - PART I

KEY: Identify the different types of real estate

There are five types of real estate:

Commercial **Residential** **Industrial**

Special Purpose **Agricultural**

PART I: For each description below, pick a real estate type that matches.

1. ______________________ **real estate** deals with land used to produce crops and raise livestock.

2. ______________________ **real estate** is real estate designed for a particular purpose.

3. ______________________ **real estate** is property used for business.

4. ______________________ **real estate** is used to manufacture products.

5. ______________________ **real estate** generally refers to property meant for people to reside or live in.

REAL ESTATE TYPES – PART II

Add the name of each real estate type to the pictures below:

Industrial **Commercial** **Agricultural**
Special Purpose **Residential**

EXAMPLES OF REAL ESTATE TYPES
(Figure 1)

FILL IN THE BLANK

DID YOU KNOW?

"Buying property at a younger age helps to build up

____

at an older age."

REAL ESTATE WORDS SEARCH

KEY: Familiarize yourself with real estate terms

Find and circle the following real estate words in the word search puzzle below:

wealth	keys	asset
homeowner	equity	mortgage
commercial	residential	money

D	E	X	D	P	J	A	I	C	S	G	N	L	Z	V	H	P	A
T	U	Z	U	D	Y	O	L	F	K	I	N	P	E	G	A	R	G
G	T	D	T	E	N	I	H	C	A	M	E	H	T	A	X	C	N
O	W	E	A	L	T	H	O	T	L	C	A	L	F	O	R	O	I
A	P	B	S	O	D	O	F	N	G	R	W	H	R	R	U	M	Y
T	N	O	S	X	Z	M	O	R	T	G	A	G	E	L	D	M	T
E	O	T	E	W	K	E	Q	U	I	T	Y	N	T	H	C	E	D
E	P	S	T	Q	H	O	W	N	E	R	S	H	I	P	P	R	U
R	A	O	E	Z	E	W	C	H	K	S	F	R	F	R	S	C	S
B	A	K	R	M	O	N	E	Y	F	R	N	T	H	N	G	I	L
S	T	O	T	X	K	E	Y	S	B	O	T	I	K	A	W	A	I
T	K	E	Y	S	T	R	E	S	I	D	E	N	T	I	A	L	N
C	Z	L	S	L	B	J	K	D	S	C	K	T	A	D	R	W	N
H	S	E	A	H	E	L	D	A	R	N	S	S	M	O	F	N	D
A	Q	N	R	K	I	K	O	M	A	T	S	I	N	G	B	O	L
P	R	I	A	T	T	H	Q	I	K	B	R	W	N	F	X	J	O

NOTES

NOTES

CHAPTER TWO

BLACK HOMEOWNERSHIP MATTERS

Real Estate and Racism

REAL ESTATE AND RACISM QUESTIONS FOR DISCUSSION

KEY: Understand the history and impacts of housing discrimination.

In your own words, answers the questions below.

1. Where does majority of Black wealth come from amongst homeowners?

___

___

___

2. What is the phrase, "40 acres and a mule," about?

___

___

___

3. What is redlining?

___

___

___

4. What is blockbusting?

___

___

___

5. How does housing discrimination affect the Black community?

___

___

FILL IN THE BLANK

Who Got the Keys in the US?

_______________ is a key to build wealth. Yet Blacks have the ______ rate of homeownership and wealth.

Rate of Homeownership by Race

BLACKS	WHITES	HISPANICS	OTHER RACES
44.1%	74.5%	49.1%	56.3%

— US Census Bureau 2020

Rate of Homeownership Before Age 35 by Race

BLACKS	WHITES	HISPANICS	ASIAN
10.8%	35%	22.7%	24.1 %

— NAREB, 2020 State of Housing in Black America Report

Median Net Worth Per Race

(what you____ minus what you____)

BLACKS	WHITES	HISPANICS	OTHER RACES
$24,100	$188,200	$36,100	$74,500

— Federal Reserves, 2019 Survey of Consumer Finances

REDLINING - PART 1

KEY: Know the history and impact of redlining.

In your own words, answer the questions below. Consider having a group discussion regarding your answers.

1. In 1934, why did the federal government create the Federal Housing Administration (FHA)?

2. What was the purpose of the New Deal program? What about the Home Owner's Loan Corporation program?

3. Were Blacks included in these two programs?

4. Do you think everyone should have the right to obtain a loan to buy property that is solely based on their ability to meet certain financial qualifications and standards, and not their race? If so, why or why not?

5. What are present day effects of redlining?

REDLINING – PART II

Lenders were allowed to use a color-coded map to indicate the race and/or financial class that predominantly resided in a particular community to reject, deny, or charge higher fees to residents in predominantly Black or Brown communities. *Search "Redlining map" on the internet to get a better idea of what it looked like.

Instructions: Match the colors and descriptions used on redlining maps.

Colors: RED BLUE YELLOW GREEN

- __________: The best communities in high demand where professional White people lived.
- __________: Still desirable and stable communities where Whites lived.
- __________: Definitely declining communities that bordered Black communities and were at risk of foreign-born, negro, or "low-grade" populations moving in.
- __________: Hazardous communities where the majority of the Black and Brown people lived, regardless of their financial status.

("The History of Redlining" from www.thoughtco.com)

Instructions: Match the colors with race that predominantly resided in the communities you identified above.

Colors: RED BLUE YELLOW GREEN

- ____________________ professional White people lived.
- ____________________ Whites lived.
- ____________________ risk of foreign-born, negro, or "low-grade" populations moving in.
- ____________________majority of the Black and Brown people lived, regardless of their financial status.

SOLUTIONS TO PROGRESS

KEY: Discuss and understand why Black homeownership matters.

1. What is the Fair Housing Act?

2. Name the historic real estate organization whose mission is equality in housing and to increase Black homeownership.

3. Why does Black homeownership matter to you?

4. What solutions do you think will help to increase the rate of Black homeownership?

NOTES

NOTES

CHAPTER THREE

BUYING UP THE BLOCK

Real Estate Investing 101

BUYING UP THE BLOCK QUESTIONS FOR DISCUSSION

1. What is the goal of a real estate investor?

2. What is a real estate exit strategy?

3. Is one real estate strategy better than another? why or why not?

4. What is an example of a holding cost?

5. What does ARV stand for?

6. What does PITI stand for?

REAL ESTATE EXIT STRATEGIES

KEY: Identify the real estate strategies and how to calculate the profits from each transaction.

Buy & Hold **Wholesaling** **Seller Finance** **Fix & Flip**

1. Investors find a property and rehabs it to later sale for a higher price. The key is to find a property that the investor can buy and rehab because the after-repair value (ARV) will be higher. In essence, the total cost to buy and repair the property is less than the price to sell it. Additionally, investors must be mindful of the expenses they have to pay to hold the property until it is sold; this is called holding cost.
   Which exit strategy is this? ______________________________

Calculate the profit: Angela is an investor that finds a property to rehab with the following costs:

$70,000 - Purchasing price

$30,000 - Amount paid to rehab

$6,000 - Holding cost

$7,300 - Closing cost

$____________ - *What is the total cost of all these expenses together?*

Three months later, Angela sells the same house at the after-repair value of $195,000. How much did Angela profit from this investment?

(FORMULA: ARV - Total cost = Profit) ______________________

2. The owner/investor will allow a buyer to pay them monthly payments to purchase their property, as opposed to the buyer taking out a loan with a bank or lending institution. In essence, the seller acts as the lender. Which exit strategy is this? ______________________________

Calculate the profit: Victor's exit strategy is to sell his property, which he doesn't owe any debts on, and serve as the lender to qualified buyer, Sean. As such, they negotiate the sales price for the property and the monthly payments for Sean to cover the loan amount, insurance, property taxes, and interest. Sean has to pay Victor $1200 a month, from which $750 is for the loan amount.

How much does Victor profit in a year from the payments? ______________

3. Investors purchase an income-producing property and rent it out to others. When deciding to do this, an investor should do a property analysis to determine how much income and profit the property will generate on a monthly and annual basis; a property analysis.
   Which exit strategy is this? ______________________________

Calculate the profit: Paul is an investor who wants to purchase a two-unit property. He will take out a loan to buy the property with a $7,000 annual debt service (principal amount owed on the housing loan). As such, he runs an analysis on the property to see how much cash he will profit:

$37,000 - Total annual revenue/income

$10,500 - Total annual operating expenses

$______________ - What is the net operating income (NOI)? (Formula: income - expenses)

$______________ - What is the cash flow? (Formula: NOI - annual debt service amount)

4. This investor finds property owners who are willing to sell their homes for less than what their properties are worth. Then the investor signs a purchasing contract with the homeowner. Next, the investor finds another investor who is willing and able to buy that same property "as is" (in its current condition and without additional repairs being made) for cash right away but for a higher price and keeps the difference.
   Which exit strategy is this? ______________________________

Calculate the profit: Jamila has a contract to buy Deborah's house for $43,000. Then she gets John, an investor, to agree to buy this same property as is for $54,000 in cash. One the same day that she buys Deborah's house, John immediately buys it from her.

As a result, how much does Jamila profit? ______________________

NAME THAT INCOME TYPE

KEY: Identify the income types that you can make from investing in real estate, depending on your exit strategy.

Write which type of income each exit strategy generates:

ACTIVE INCOME **PASSIVE INCOME** **INTEREST INCOME**

Exit Strategy	Income Type
Seller Finance	
Fix & Flip	
Wholesale	
Buy & Hold	

ACQUIRING REAL ESTATE WORD SCRAMBLE

KEY: Learn the various methods to acquiring real estate.

Unscrambled the real estate words below to identify each method.

______________ 1. **laeR tatEes lmentvesnt usTrt (REIT):** You can invest in a company that buys and manages income-producing real estate and allows others (shareholders) to invest in the company without having to buy and manage the property themselves but still generate a profit.

______________ 2. **Txa ieLsn:** You can pay someone's delinquent tax bill at a county with the possibility of becoming the new owner or getting reimbursed with interested after a certain period of time.

______________ 3. **eRnt ot wOn (lease option):** You can rent a property until you are able to buy it from the owner. In essence you are making monthly payments with a portion towards rent and a portion toward purchasing the property.

______________ 4. **alradiTtion eomH ingurchPas:** You can buy a property from an owner outright by paying all cash or taking out a loan from a bank or lending institution. After a series of events (see flowchart: 12 Steps to Securing the Keys), the lender pays the seller the full purchasing price as agreed between the seller and buyer, the deed is transferred to the buyer as the new owner, and then the buyer begins to make monthly payments to reimburse the lender (if they didn't pay cash) for the loan. The process may vary by state.

KEYS TO CREDIT

KEY: Understand that each lender has their own processes and qualifications to get a mortgage loan from them. Nevertheless, all lenders tend to look at the 5 Cs of credit (trustworthiness to repay for products and service given before paying) to assess your financial status. Together, the 5 Cs of credit make up your credit (a.k.a. FICO) score. Building and maintaining good credit is a key to being approved for mortgage loans.

PART I. What are the 5 Cs of Credit?

capi ________________ capa ________________ col ________________

cre ________________ cha ________________

PART II. Your FICO score (credit score), is developed over time and is based on the five factors below:

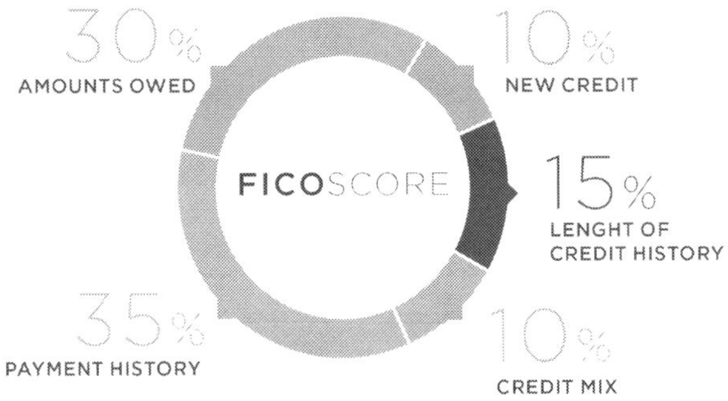

Fill in the blanks with the following:

Credit History **Payment History** **Credit Mix**
Credit Utilization **New Credit**

1. ______________________ - the amount of debt owed
2. ______________________ - how long the debt is owed
3. ______________________ - the different types of credit accounts opened
4. ______________________ - the number of new credit accounts opened and inquiries from credit applications to companies
5. ______________________ - how often you make payments on time (the most important factor in determining your credit score)

CREDITWORTHINESS

Part III. Everyone is given a credit score, ranging from 300 to 800, to rate their creditworthiness. Creditworthiness indicates how worthy you are to receive products or services before paying for them. The higher your credit score, the easier it will be to get loans for lower interest rates and fees to buy real estate or other products.

CREDIT SCORE CHART

Questions for discussion:

1. Name one way to keep your credit score high.

   ____

2. What's the highest credit score you can have?

   ____

3. What rating is a 635 credit score considered?

   ____

BUDGETING 101 - PART I

A budget is a projection of your income minus your expenses to be a good steward over your finances.

KEY: Understand how to create a budget based on making your needs a priority over your wants.

Identify what your NEEDS (N) are versus your WANTS (W)

1. ____________ $90 Fourth pair of shoes
2. ____________ $950 Mortgage/rental payment
3. ____________ $230 Groceries
4. ____________ $220 Transportation to school or work
5. ____________ $130 Hang out with friends
6. ____________ $110 Hygiene (deodorant, soap, tooth paste, lotion, etc.)
7. ____________ $75 Uniform for school or work
8. ____________ $220 Fast food twice a week
9. ____________ $450 Brand name bag
10. ____________ $225 Money in savings
11. ____________ $125 Concert ticket
12. ____________ $75 Phone bill
13. ____________ $90 New game for PlayStation
14. ____________ $100 Credit card bill

Total amount for Needs: ____________

Total amount for Wants: ____________

BUDGETING 101 – PART II

Based on your expenses that you need to pay each month, create your own budget based on a monthly income of $1900 a month

Income: $1900

Expenses (Based on needs only, use more space if needed)

- ______________
- ______________
- ______________
- ______________
- ______________

Add your total expenses up.

Total expenses = $ ______________

Total income minus total expenses = $ ______________

Do you have money left over? Yes or No

If YES, what "wants" do you want to include in your budget now? (These may change monthly.)

- ______________
- ______________
- ______________
- ______________
- ______________

If NO, you need to make adjustments to your budget to ensure all the needs are paid for first. The goal is to always take care of your needs first and only use a portion of the money left over—if any—for your wants afterwards. This will help build your credit and become financially disciplined in life.

12 STEPS TO SECURE THE KEYS TO HOMEOWNERSHIP

KEY: To know the process of buying property.

Instructions: Put the steps to buying a property in order based on the process provided in the book. Place the number on the blanks provided.

Reminders: These steps are after securing funding to buy a property. They may slightly vary by state.

_______ *Transaction gets cleared to close*

_______ *Submit earnest money*

_______ *Get a comparative (a.k.a. market) analysis*

_______ *Appraiser determine property value*

_______ *Consult with a real estate agent (R' Legacy Realty)*

_______ *Submit an offer to the seller*

_______ *Conduct a final walkthrough*

_______ *Conduct a Home Inspection*

_______ *Get property listings and start house shopping*

_______ *Choose a property to put an offer on*

_______ *Send signed copies of the contract to team*

_______ *A title search is conducted*

NOTES

NOTES

CHAPTER FOUR

ACT LIKE A TEEN BUT THINK LIKE A BOSS

Managing Real Estate

ACT LIKE A TEEN BUT THINK LIKE A BOSS QUESTIONS FOR DISCUSSION

1. What is a boss?

____

____

____

2. Why is character important to being successful?

____

____

____

3. Real estate is a people driven industry. (Circle your answer below.)

   TRUE *FALSE*

4. How you treat and service others will not affect your reputation nor ability to get the opportunities. (Circle your answer below.)

   TRUE *FALSE*

5. Fill in the blanks:

   Even at your ______________ and stage in life, you don't need a boss ______________ to have a boss mentality and ______________.

NEXT-LEVEL BOSS BEHAVIOR

KEY: Learn and demonstrate the qualifies of a next-level boss.

A boss is someone who's in charge. But being just a boss is not enough—a boss who makes a positive impact on the lives of others is next level.

Let's look at the qualities below to select if it is Boss (B) or Next-Level Boss (NLB) behavior.

1. ________ Has authority to tell others what to do
2. ________ Inspires and encourages their team to be their best
3. ________ Is reliable and dependable, honoring other people's time
4. ________ Evaluates the team's work performance
5. ________ Does not need validation from others to determine their value
6. ________ Hires and fires people to work for the company
7. ________ Is not perfect, but takes responsibility and accountability for their actions
8. ________ Has integrity because their words and actions are the same

SKILLS SETS MIX AND MATCH

KEY: Unlock skill sets of a next-level boss in real estate, which are also useful in all career fields.

Instructions: Mix and match the skill sets with its correct description by drawing a connecting line.

Customer service skills	Ability to manage appointments and paperwork, maintain a scheduling and filing system while meeting deadlines.
Critical thinking skills	Being open and able to discuss your products, services, and the industry, as well as listen to your customers' and team members' needs and feedback.
Communication skills	Respectfully working with other professionals to effectively run the business and service your clients.
Computer skills	Able to quickly think of the most effective way to solve problems (which is why it is important to be well educated about the industry to know updated rules, regulations, strategies, and the processes allowed to solve them).
Organizational skills	Having basic computer skills; being active on social media; and staying updated on new real estate apps, websites, and systems.
Team player skills	Being flexible, respectful, and knowledgeable while keeping the customer's needs a priority. Aiming to exceed your customer's expectations before, during, and after a transaction. How you treat customers will affect your reputation

FILL IN THE BLANKS

"Even as a ____ you are a ____ because you are in charge of your thoughts, words, and actions."

Mia Rogers

PROPERTY MANAGER JOB DESCRIPTION

KEY: Understand the role and duties of a property manager.

Remember, the level of responsibility when managing someone else's property may vary depending on the owner's needs, and there should be a written agreement reflecting the specific tasks and pay rate.

Instructions: Image you were looking to hire a property manager. Write up a job description for others to understand the position you are hiring for.

1. What is the role of a property manager?

___

___

___

2. What is the goal of a property manager?

___

___

___

3. List at least seven responsibilities of property manager based on the book.

   Example: Ensure the property is always clean, safe and sanitary

- ___
- ___
- ___
- ___
- ___
- ___
- ___

NOTES

NOTES

CHAPTER FIVE

ONE KEY UNLOCKS MANY DOORS

Careers in Real Estate

ONE KEY UNLOCKS MANY DOORS QUESTIONS FOR DISCUSSION

1. Why is real estate the one key that unlocks many doors?

____

____

____

2. Who is your favorite real estate professional? Why?

____

____

____

3. Do real estate requirements vary by state? (Circle your answer below.)

TRUE ***FALSE***

4. Can you be a real estate agent in multiple states at the same time? (Circle your answer below.)

TRUE ***FALSE***

NAME THAT R.E.P (REAL ESTATE PROFESSIONAL)

KEY: Understand the various careers and responsibilities of real estate professionals.

Instructions: Based on the description, name which R.E.P it describes and select from the options below:

Agent	Lender	Attorney	Home Inspector
Developer	Instructor	Home Inspector	Sponsoring Broker
Appraiser	Insurance agent	Property Manager	Managing Broker
Investor	Title Agent	General Contractor	

Example: Invests in real estate to make money. This type of R.E.P. may buy property individually or with others. This type of R.E.P. completes various financial and property analyses to determine how profitable a property is before they decide to spend their money and time on it. **Answer:** Investor

1. ______________________ A person who teaches real estate courses on various real estate topics; they may also write lesson plans and curriculum for the classes.

2. ______________________ Specializes on the legal aspects of the real estate transaction.

3. ______________________ The main licensed labor worker who oversees other contractors and building project at a construction site.

4. ______________________ A licensed individual who works to help others to buy, sell, or rent out a property. This type of R.E.P. helps negotiate deals and monitor the process to help their client(s) to get to the closing stage, which is the final step to transfer ownership or leasing of a property.

5. ______________________ Oversees properties for themselves and/or others—also known as a landlord.

6. ______________________ A licensed professional that thoroughly examines the entire property to evaluate its condition.

7. ______________________ An individual who is licensed to help residential property owners to rent out their properties and tenants to find residential properties to rent out.

8. ______________________ A real estate company that real estate agents and managing brokers must work under to hold their license.

9. ______________________ Plans and creates ideas for new real estate developments or for renovating existing real estate. Many are also architects or work with architects to draw a detailed design of the projects.

10. ______________________ A licensed professional who assesses a property to determine its value.

11. ______________________ Real estate agents who are licensed to manage a real estate company and other agents.

12. ______________________ Provides various types of homeowners and rental insurance.

13. ______________________ A person or company that loans money to purchase, repair, or rehab a property.

BONUS: Title agent - A neutral party in the real estate transaction that ensures the title of property is cleared to transfer to a new owner(s). The title company assigns an agent to research the history of ownership of a property and help to provide buyers with title insurance to cover them in case any issues of ownership come up after they buy the property.

FILL IN THE BLANK

Investor *Agent* *Manager*

"You can earn
__________ & __________
sources of __________
within the real
estate industry!"

Lender *Inspector* *Attorney*

R' LEGACY CASE STUDY

Instructions: Based on the case study, name which title (mentioned in the REP activity) describes each character.

Activity: Role play and act out the scenarios, while others guest the roles. Also, create your own scenarios based on the roles as well.

The Rogers family consists of generations of real estate professionals and investors. They all work together to build a legacy and create generational wealth by investing in real estate. John teaches his family and others about various real estate topics and encourages them to obtain a real estate license. Steve is the financer of all of the real estate deals that the family buys and they have to pay him back with interest. Malcolm is licensed to help others to buy and sell properties in various states. Meanwhile, Paul is the main labor contractor and oversees other contractors to ensure the properties are properly rehabbed. Together, the family started a company called R' Legacy Realty that hires other real estate agents to work under their office. As such, Donna manages all of the family properties as well as other real estate agents. Lastly, Akilah takes care of all of the legal paperwork for the real estate transactions.

1. The entire family are real estate ______________________
2. John is a ______________________
3. Steve is a ______________________
4. Donna is a ______________ and ______________
5. Malcolm is a ______________________
6. Paul is a ______________________
7. Akilah is a ______________________
8. R' Legacy Realty is the ______________________

NOTES

NOTES

CHAPTER SIX

OWNERSHIP MINDSET

The Business of Real Estate

OWNERSHIP MINDSET QUESTIONS FOR DISCUSSION

1. Why is having an ownership mindset important?

2. In general, property owners have a higher financial status than renters. (Circle your answer below.)

   TRUE *FALSE*

3. All bosses are also owners. (Circle your answer below.)

   TRUE *FALSE*

4. All owners are also bosses. (Circle your answer below.)

   TRUE *FALSE*

5. What is a business plan?

6. What are the four Ps the marketing mix?

7. What does SWOT stand for?

8. Why is it important to understand finances in business?

FILL IN THE BLANKS

DID YOU KNOW?

"______ have net worth 40x HIGHER than ______"

- Federal Reserves 2020

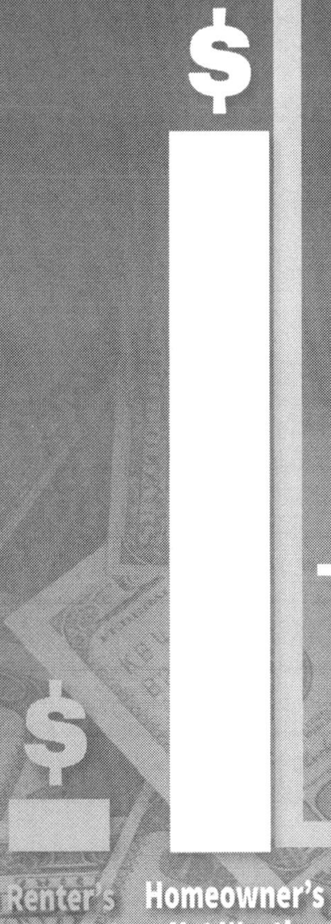

BUSINESS PLAN MIX AND MATCH

KEY: Understand the components of a business plan.

Instructions: Business owners in all industries should have a business plan. Read and identify the descriptions of the business components. Draw a line to indicate which components match the descriptions.

COMPONENTS

Executive Summary

Business Description

Organization

Financial Plan

Marketing Plan

DESCRIPTION

A breakdown of the money that your company projects and actually makes (revenue/income) and spends (expenses).

A strategy for how you will communicate the value of your product/service to the public, particularly your customers.

A summary of your business plan with the main keys from each section.

Details about your team members, partnerships, processes, and systems.

A detailed description of your company, which should include the concept of your company, your company goals, accomplishments, the mission statement, and vision statement.

FINANCIAL STATEMENTS WORD SEARCH PUZZLE

KEY: Understand the various financial statement in a business plan.

Instructions: Identify the correct financial statement with its description and find it in the word search puzzle

Activity: Go on the internet to search for examples of each type of financial statement.

T	U	Z	U	D	Y	O	L	F	K	I	E	P	S	T	Y	N	G
G	T	D	I	N	P	B	A	L	A	N	C	E	S	H	E	E	T
O	A	M	M	E	H	U	A	X	L	C	B	A	K	S	F	R	I
A	P	B	C	A	L	D	O	R	G	R	S	T	O	R	N	T	Y
T	N	O	R	W	H	G	R	U	B	F	T	H	Y	E	O	T	T
E	I	N	C	O	M	E	S	T	A	T	E	M	E	N	T	B	D
E	P	S	T	Y	N	T	H	C	E	R	H	S	E	A	H	E	U
R	A	O	L	B	J	K	D	S	C	K	T	Q	N	R	K	I	S
B	A	K	H	E	L	D	A	R	N	S	S	R	I	A	T	T	L
S	T	C	A	S	H	F	L	O	W	S	I	I	K	A	W	A	I
T	H	Y	T	T	H	Q	I	K	B	R	W	M	O	F	N	D	N

Types of Financial Statements/Reports:

Budget **Income Statement** **Cash Flow** **Balance Sheet**

1. ____________ Report of the actual cash that flows in and out of the company each month. This is the most important statement because it tells you how much cash the company has on hand.
2. ____________ Projection of the income and expenses from your business.
3. ____________ Report of your company's assets (things that add value, such as real estate) versus liabilities (things that take away value, such as a mortgage payment) to determine the equity (assets minus liabilities).
4. ____________ Report of the actual breakdown of the income and expenses from your business.

MISSION and VISION STATEMENT

KEY: Have a clear mission of what you want do to and why

Instructions: Write out what your real estate need is, then a clear mission and vision statement based on fulling that need. This can be a personal real estate goal for you and your family and/or the public.

Example:

NEED: To increase the rate of black homeownership and wealth because it is the lowest amongst all races. (Based on my research)

MY MISSION: To expose and educate today's black teens in real estate to become tomorrow's homeowners and investor.
(This is the purpose of my book and classes)

MY VISION: More black youth develop an ownership mindset and are empowered to obtain generational wealth through real estate.
(This is the impact I hope to make in the future from my mission)

NEED:

____

____

____

MISSION STATEMENT:

____

____

____

VISION STATEMENT:

____

____

____

NOTES

NOTES

USE YOUR KEY

How to Get Started NOW

REAL ESTATE GOALS

KEY: Develop a roadmap and action plan to intentionally prepare to build wealth through real estate.

Instructions: Based on your mission/vision, write out your real estate goals. Goals are important to help you create a roadmap of your success. Your goals should be SMART: Specific, Measurable, Achievable, Realistic, and Timely. For each goal, write the plan of action to achieve it, the resources needed, and the time frame to complete it. It's okay if your goals change over time; you must start somewhere.

My Example:

MY GOAL: Teach at least one real estate class at a predominantly Black youth organization/school per month.

TIMEFRAME: Starting January 2022 until December 2024

PLAN OF ACTION: Send out invitations and proposals to youth organizations to schedule a session(s).

RESOURCES NEEDED: A team, transportation, venues, teaching materials, computer and books.

Example for youth:

GOAL: To save up $100

TIMEFRAME: By the end of 2021

PLAN OF ACTION: Save 5% of my allowance, birthday, and holiday money to put in my savings account.

RESOURCES NEEDED: Savings account set up by my parent/guardian, money, and a budget

YOUR GOALS

#1 GOAL

TIMEFRAME

PLAN OF ACTION

RESOURCES NEEDED

#2 GOAL

TIMEFRAME

PLAN OF ACTION

RESOURCES NEEDED

#3 GOAL

TIMEFRAME

PLAN OF ACTION

RESOURCES NEEDED

#4 GOAL

TIMEFRAME

PLAN OF ACTION

RESOURCES NEEDED

AFFIRMATIONS FOR GENERATIONAL WEALTH

KEY: Intentionally speak positive words to manifest the reality to become a homeowner and/or real estate investor.

Instructions: Take your real estate goals and write out positive statements (a.k.a. affirmations) to declare them into your reality. Your affirmations will help you develop an ownership mindset and determination to build a legacy of wealth for you and your family through real estate.

Example: (Based on my goal from the previous activity)
Affirmation: "I have earned and saved enough money to purchase profitable real estate."

AFFIRMATION #1

Write it:

____

____

Believe it and declare it out loud daily!

AFFIRMATION #2

Write it:

____

____

Believe it and declare it out loud daily!

AFFIRMATION #3

Write it:

____

____

Believe it and declare it out loud daily!

AFFIRMATION #4

Write it:

____

____

Believe it and declare it out loud daily!

PASS THE KEYS

KEY: Use your knowledge about real estate to empower someone else.

Instructions: Commit to building generational wealth within your family and community members by sharing this book of knowledge with your peers, younger siblings, cousins, and friends. Some may take the keys of information, while others may resist them, but as long as you offer this information to others, you have done your part.

First, list three things that you learned about real estate from the *Who Got the Key? Building Generational Wealth through Real Estate* book.

1. ______________________________

2. ______________________________

3. ______________________________

Next, list at least three people that you commit to passing these keys of information about real estate to:

Name: ______________________________

Role: ______________________________

Name: ______________________________

Role: ______________________________

Name: ______________________________

Role: ______________________________

INTERESTED IN BECOMING A REAL ESTATE AGENT?

Apply for a real estate scholarship. Do you want to become a real estate agent? It's possible! In some states, you can become a real estate agent at the age of 18 or 21 with a high school diploma or GED. The age, cost, and classes required to obtain a real estate license may vary by state. Research online real estate scholarships in your state for funding opportunities to take the real estate classes. Many real estate associations and states have funds specifically for minorities such as the National Association of Real Estate Brokers (NAREB) and the National Association of Realtors.

JOHN P. ROGERS
Real Estate Foundation

My siblings and I started the *John P. Rogers Real Estate Foundation* to honor our father, who gave us the keys to real estate investing. We will continue his legacy by providing scholarships to black teens to obtain a real estate license.

Eligibility:

- Residing in Illinois or Indiana
- Ages 18 21 only
- Earned a high school diploma or GED
- Has read the *Who Got the Keys book and completed the workbook*

For more information, visit **www.whogotthekeys.com** or **www.rlegacyrealty.com**.

REAL ESTATE WEALTH BUILDER PLEDGE

I ______________________________ (Name), pledge to use my keys of information about real estate to prepare to secure the keys to homeownership and real estate investments. I pledge to become a student of the industry to continuously learn about real estate to make well-informed decisions. I pledge to implement my plans of action to reach my real estate goals. As I am empowered, I pledge to empower others by passing the keys of real estate to my peers and the next generations because I am a generational wealth builder through real estate.

*Take a selfie with a key to remind yourself of your pledge.

NOTES

NOTES

CHAPTER 1 - Keeping It Real About Real Estate & Wealth
KEY SHEET

PAGE 2 - QUESTIONS FOR DISCUSSION

1. To give access, unlock something
2. Land plus improvements
3. Individuals, families, businesses, organizations and/or the government
4. Build wealth, rights to access, exclude, dissolve, enjoy it.
5. Something that adds value
6. Abundance of money, riches
7. Abundance of money, good health, and peace of mind
8. Build more wealth sooner

PAGE 3 - REAL ESTATE TYPES - PART I

1. Agricultural
2. Special purpose
3. Commercial
4. Industrial
5. Residential

PAGE 4 - REAL ESTATE TYPES - PART II

(Based on order of photos)

Residential
Commercial
Agricultural
Industrial
Special Purpose

PAGE 5 - FILL IN THE BLANK: more wealth

PAGE 6 - REAL ESTATE WORD SEARCH PUZZLE

T	U	Z	U	D	Y	O	L	F	K	I	N	P	E	G	A	R	G
G	T	D	T	E	N	I	H	C	A	M	E	H	T	A	X	**C**	N
O	**W**	**E**	**A**	**L**	**T**	**H**	O	T	L	C	A	L	F	O	R	**O**	I
A	P	B	**S**	O	D	**O**	F	N	G	R	W	H	R	R	U	**M**	Y
T	N	O	**S**	X	Z	**M**	**O**	**R**	**T**	**G**	**A**	**G**	**E**	L	D	**M**	T
E	O	T	**E**	W	K	**E**	**Q**	**U**	**I**	**T**	**Y**	N	T	H	C	**E**	D
E	P	S	**T**	Q	H	**O**	W	N	E	R	S	H	I	P	P	**R**	U
R	A	O	E	Z	E	**W**	C	H	K	S	F	R	F	R	S	**C**	S
B	A	K	R	**M**	**O**	**N**	**E**	**Y**	F	R	N	T	H	N	G	**I**	L
S	T	O	T	X	K	**E**	Y	S	B	O	T	I	K	A	W	**A**	I
T	**K**	**E**	**Y**	**S**	T	**R**	**E**	**S**	**I**	**D**	**E**	**N**	**T**	**I**	**A**	**L**	N
C	Z	L	S	L	B	J	K	D	S	C	K	T	A	D	R	W	N

CHAPTER 2 - Black Homeownership Matters KEY SHEET

PAGE 10 - QUESTIONS FOR DISCUSSION

1. Owning real estate
2. The order, known as "40 acres and a mule", allowed former slaves to each own up to 40 acres of land and a mule (also known as a donkey), which farmers use for transportation and to carry supplies.
3. Redlining is when lenders discriminate on loan applications by refusing to lend to someone or charging higher rates and fees based on the person's race or ethnicity, or within certain communities
4. Pursuing others to relocate out of a neighborhood because as shift of minorities moving in will cause their housing values to decrease.
5. Discrimination negatively affected Blacks' ability to build wealth at the same rate and level as other races.

PAGE 11 - FILL IN THE BLANK: (based on the image): Homeownership, Blacks, own, owe

PAGE 12 - REDLINING - PART I

1. To restore the housing market after the Great Depression as the economy as a whole suffered.
2. The New Deal program provided incentives and financial assistance to help people to become new homeowners. The HOLC program helped current homeowners to refinance (redo the loan for better rates) their current mortgage loan.
3. No.
4. (Your opinion.)
5. Lack of resources, quality education, hospitals, and housing in predominantly Black communities.

PAGE 13 - REDLINING - PART II

Top portion:	1. Green	2. Blue	3. Yellow	4. Red
Bottom portion:	1. Green	2. Blue	3. Yellow	4. Red

PAGE 14 - SOLUTIONS TO PROGRESS

1. Prohibits race and color discrimination in regards to the rental or sale of housing. *Also includes: sex, religion, national origin, disability, familial status (pregnant or having kids under 18)
2. National Association of Real Estate Brokers (NAREB), there are different chapters in each state.
3. (Your opinion.)
4. (Your opinion.)

CHAPTER 3 - Buying Up the Block
KEY SHEET

PAGE 18 - QUESTIONS FOR DISCUSSION

1. Make money and impact.
2. Purpose and plan for investing in real estate once you buy it.
3. No, various strategies work for different people for different reasons.
4. Mortgage, any utility bill, taxes, and homeowners' association bills.
5. After Repair Value
6. Principal, Interest, Taxes, and Insurance. These may all make up your mortgage payment.

PAGE 19 - REAL ESTATE STRATEGIES

1. Fix and Flip, $113,300, $81,700
2. Seller's Finance, $14,400 ($1200 monthly x 12 [for number of months in a year])
3. Buy and Hold, $26,500, $19,500
4. Wholesale, $11,000

PAGE 22 - NAME THAT INCOME TYPE

1. Interest income
2. Active Income
3. Active Income
4. Passive Income

PAGE 23 - ACQUIRING REAL ESTATE WORD SCRAMBLE

1. Real Estate Investment Trust
2. Tax Liens
3. Rent to Own
4. Traditional Home Purchasing

PAGE 24 - KEYS TO CREDIT

PART I Capital, capacity, collateral, credit, character

PART II

1. Credit Utilization
2. Credit History
3. Credit Mix
4. New Credit
5. Payment History

PAGE 25 - CREDITWORTHINESS - QUESTIONS FOR DISCUSSION

1. Pay your bills on time, don't apply for nor take out a lot of loans, stay within your budget, keep credit card balance low (under 30%), etc.
2. 850 credit score is the highest.
3. 635 credit score is a fair credit score.

PAGE 26 - BUDGETING 101

PART I

1. W
2. N
3. N
4. N
5. W
6. N
7. N
8. W
9. W
10. N
11. W
12. N
13. W
14. N

Total Needs: $1985

Wants: $1105

PART II

Based on the budget you set for yourself, the goal is to ensure all your needs are paid on time first. Then adjust the amounts of the wants according to your preferences.

Tip: Don't spend all of your money left over on wants, if any. Always save and keep emergency money available.

PAGE 28 - 12 STEPS TO SECURING THE KEY

11	12
7	8
4	2
9	3
1	6
5	10

CHAPTER 4 - Act like a Teen But Think like a Boss
KEY SHEET

PAGE 32 - QUESTIONS FOR DISCUSSION

1. Someone who is in charge.
2. It can attract the right people and opportunities to reach and maintain success.
3. True
4. False
5. age, title, behavior

PAGE 33 - NEXT-LEVEL BOSS BEHAVIOR

1. B
2. N
3. N
4. B
5. N
6. B
7. N
8. N

PAGE 34 - SKILLS SET MIX AND MATCH

- **Customer service skills:** Being flexible, respectful, and knowledgeable while keeping the customer's needs a priority. Aiming to exceed your customer's expectations before, during, and after a transaction. How you treat customers will affect your reputation.
- **Critical thinking skills:** Able to quickly think of the most effective way to solve problems (which is why it is important to be well educated about the industry to know updated rules, regulations, strategies, and the processes allowed to solve them).
- **Communication skills:** Being open and able to discuss your products, services, and the industry, as well as listen to your customers' and team members' needs and feedback.
- **Computer skills:** Having basic computer skills; being active on social media; and staying updated on new real estate apps, websites, and systems.

- **Organizational skills:** Ability to manage appointments and paperwork, maintain a scheduling and filing system while meeting deadlines.
- **Team player skills:** Respectfully working with other professionals to effectively run the business and service your clients.

PAGE 35 - FILL IN THE BLANK: TEEN, BOSS

PAGE 36 - PROPERTY MANAGEMENT JOB DESCRIPTION

1. The role of a property manager is a boss who supervises and manages the day-to-day activities of real estate.

2. Prioritize the best interests of the property owner by recommending, implementing, and overseeing the most efficient systems and processes to maintain the property in the best condition for profitability.

3. Responsibilities of a property manager may include, but are not limited to:

    - Ensuring the property is always clean, safe, and sanitary
    - Collecting rental money from tenants, with a system for all tenants to submit payments the same way. KEY: Always provide customers with receipts for their payments for tracking purposes.
    - Responding to tenant questions, concerns, and requests for repairs
    - Preparing and advertising vacant units that are ready to be rented
    - Interviewing and hiring staff and contractors
    - Assigning maintenance workers to repair tasks
    - Maintaining records and filing systems
    - Providing status reports to the owner(s) to keep them updated about any changes with the property
    - Paying bills associated with the property, such as lawn care, snow removal, and repairs
    - Managing the finances for the property and creating financial reports to track the income and expenses (see Chapter 6 for more details)

CHAPTER 5 - One Key Unlocks Many Doors
KEY SHEET

PAGE 40 - QUESTIONS FOR DISCUSSION

1. There are various careers and opportunities within real estate that you can pursue to earn multiple streams of income.
2. (Your opinion.)
3. True
4. True

NAME THAT R.E.P

1. Real Estate Instructor
2. Real Estate Attorney
3. General Contractor
4. Real Estate Agent
5. Property Manager
6. Home Inspector
7. Leasing Agent
8. Sponsoring Broker
9. Real Estate Developer
10. Appraiser
11. Managing Broker
12. Insurance agent
13. Lender

PAGE 43 - FILL IN THE BLANK: unlimited, multiple

PAGE 44 - R' LEGACY CASE STUDY

1. Investors
2. Real Estate Instructor
3. Lender
4. Property Manager and Managing Broker
5. Real Estate Agent
6. General Contractor
7. Real Estate Attorney
8. Sponsoring Broker

CHAPTER 6 - Ownership Mindset
KEY SHEET

PAGE 48 - QUESTIONS FOR DISCUSSIONS

1. Mind over matter is powerful. Your thoughts have power to become your reality.
2. True
3. False
4. True
5. A roadmap of how your business will operate to make a profit
6. Product, price, place and promotion
7. Strengths, weaknesses, opportunities, and threats
8. It the most important part because without money, there is no business nor profit. You also want to avoid being taken advantage of.

PAGE 49 - FILL IN THE BLANK: Homeowners, Renters

PAGE 50 - BUSINESS PLAN MIX AND MATCH

- **Executive Summary:** A summary of your business plan with the main keys from each section. *Generally, you write this section last, though it is the first part of your business plan.*
- **Business Description:** A detailed description of your company, which should include the concept of your company, your company goals, accomplishments, the mission statement, and the vision statement
- **Organization:** Details about your team members, partnerships, processes, and systems.
- **Financial Plan:** A breakdown of the money that your company projects and actually makes (revenue/income) and spends (expenses).
- **Marketing Plan:** A strategy for how you will communicate the value of your product/service to the public, particularly your customers

PAGE 51 - FINANCIAL STATEMENTS

WORD SEARCH PUZZLE

T	U	Z	U	D	Y	O	L	F	K	I	E	P	S	T	Y	N	G
G	T	D	I	N	P	**B**	**A**	**L**	**A**	**N**	**C**	**E**	**S**	**H**	**E**	**E**	**T**
O	A	M	M	E	H	**U**	A	X	L	C	B	A	K	S	F	R	I
A	P	B	C	A	L	**D**	O	R	G	R	S	T	O	R	N	T	Y
T	N	O	R	W	H	**G**	R	U	B	F	T	H	Y	E	O	T	T
E	**I**	**N**	**C**	**O**	**M**	**E**	**S**	**T**	**A**	**T**	**E**	**M**	**E**	**N**	**T**	B	D
E	P	S	T	Y	N	**T**	H	C	E	R	H	S	E	A	H	E	U
R	A	O	L	B	J	K	D	S	C	K	T	Q	N	R	K	I	S
B	A	K	H	E	L	D	A	R	N	S	S	R	I	A	T	T	L
S	T	**C**	**A**	**S**	**H**	**F**	**L**	**O**	**W**	S	I	I	K	A	W	A	I
T	H	Y	T	T	H	Q	I	K	B	R	W	M	O	F	N	D	N

TYPES OF FINANCIAL STATEMENTS/REPORTS:

1. Cash flow
2. Budget
3. Balance sheet
4. Income Statement

PAGE 52 - MISSION AND VISION STATEMENT

Answers based on your own words.

CHAPTER 7 - Use Your Keys
KEY SHEET

PAGE 57 - YOUR GOALS

Answers are based on your own goals.

References

Allaway, Wellington J., Fillmore W. Galaty, Robert C. Kyle. *Modern Real Estate Practice in Illinois*, edited by Leo Schwartz and Martha R. Williams, JD, 10th ed Wisconsin Dearborn Real Estate Education, 2020.

Anderson, Dana, "Redlining Legacy of Inequity: $212,000 Less Home Equity, Low Homeownership Rates for Black Families," Redfin, June 11, 2020, www.redfin.com/news.

Aronowitz, Michelle, Jung Choi, Edward Golding, Morgan Green, Richard Green, Maurice Jourdain-Earl, Ashlyn A. Nelson, Vanessa Gail Perry, Lisa Rice, Lauren Rhue. "2020 State Of Housing In Black America: Challenges Facing Black Homeowners And Homebuyers During The Covid-19 Pandemic And An Agenda For Public Policy," NAREB, August 2020, https://www.nareb.com/shiba-report/.

Bhutta, Neil, Andrew C. Chang, Lisa J. Dettling, and Joanne W. Hsu (2020). "Disparities in Wealth by Race and Ethnicity in the 2019 Survey of Consumer Finances," FEDS Notes. Washington: Board of Governors of the Federal Reserve System, September 28, 2020, https://doi.org/10.17016/2380-7172.2797.

Choi, Jung Hyun, "Breaking Down the Black-White Homeownership Gap," Urban Wire (blog), Urban Institute, February 21, 2020, https://www.urban.org/urban-wire/breaking-down-black-white-homeownership-gap.

"Data USA: Real Estate Brokers and Sales Agents." *Deloitte.com.* The Census Bureau's American Community Survey (ACS) Public Use Microdata Sample (PUMS), 2017 Web. 12 January 2021. https://datausa.io/profile/soc/real-estate-brokers-sales-agents#ethnicity

Gates Jr., Henry Louis. "The African American Many Rivers to Cross: The Truth Behind 40 Acres and a Mule," PBS, 2013, https://www.pbs.org/wnet/african-americans-many-rivers-to-cross/history/the-truth-behind-40-acres-and-a-mule/.

Lockwood, Beatrix. "The History of Redlining." ThoughtCo, Dec. 16, 2020, thoughtco.com/redlining-definition-4157858.

"Quarterly Residential Vacancies and Homeownership: Fourth Quarter 2020." *Census.gov.* US Census Bureau, US Department of Commerce, 2021 Web. 7 Feb. 2021. https://www.census.gov/housing/hvs/index.html

Creative Production Credits

123rf.com - Image # 34533095 Thomas Gowanlock
Freepik - Additional photo/graphics provided
iStock By Getty Images
iStock.com/JamesPintar, iStock.com/Hikesterson, iStock.com/Rafalkrakow,
iStock.com/tonda, iStock.com/JaySi, iStock.com/Ahavelaar, iStock.com/Maksymowicz,
iStock.com/buzbuzzer, iStock.com/Ploughmann, iStock.com/TennesseePhotographer,
iStock.com/fstop123.

www.whogotthekeys.com
www.rlegacyrealty.com
IG: @realtordonnajr
FB: facebook.com/realtordonnajr